eBay

The Ultimate Step-By-Step Beginners Guide to Sell on eBay and Build a Successful Business Empire from Scratch

Table of Contents

Introduction

eBay: The Basics

Getting ready to $ell

Think before you start Selling

Business on eBay is Fun!

Some tips and strategies

A Few Insights and secrets from established sellers

The secrets of branding and marketing

Staying safe from scams

Conclusion

Free Bonus

© **Copyright 2016 by Mark Thomas - All rights reserved.**

This document is geared towards providing exact and reliable information in regards to the topic and issue covered. The publication is sold with the idea that the publisher is not required to render accounting, officially permitted, or otherwise, qualified services. If advice is necessary, legal or professional, a practiced individual in the profession should be ordered.

- From a Declaration of Principles which was accepted and approved equally by a Committee of the American Bar Association and a Committee of Publishers and Associations.

In no way is it legal to reproduce, duplicate, or transmit any part of this document in either electronic means or in printed format. Recording of this publication is strictly prohibited and any storage of this document is not allowed unless with written permission from the publisher. All rights reserved.

The information provided herein is stated to be truthful and consistent, in that any liability, in terms of inattention or otherwise, by any usage or abuse of any policies, processes, or directions contained within is the solitary and utter responsibility of the recipient reader. Under no circumstances will any legal responsibility or blame be held against the publisher for any reparation, damages, or monetary loss due to the information herein, either directly or indirectly.

Respective authors own all copyrights not held by the publisher.

The information herein is offered for informational purposes solely, and is universal as so. The presentation of the information is without contract or any type of guarantee assurance.

The trademarks that are used are without any consent, and the publication of the trademark is without permission or backing by the trademark owner. All trademarks and brands within this book are for clarifying purposes only and are the owned by the owners themselves, not affiliated with this document.

Introduction

Back in the late 90s, at the beginning of the dot com bubble, a man named Pierre Omidyar founded an online platform called AuctionWeb. Back then it was kind of an online fair for collectors who bought and sold various items online via bidding and auction. But within a decade, ActionWeb transformed itself, rebranded as eBay and become the Giant multi-billion dollar e-commerce site where literally anyone, from 20-year-old college kid to 40-year-old mums can sell any kind of goods online. eBay soon became THE platform for professional online retailers worldwide spanning its operations in more than 30 countries.

For the past two decades, millions of people are using eBay to earn some extra cash or to sell unused items which could be useful to others who are looking for it. There are people whose first introduction to eBay happened when they were clearing their room and found old vinyl LP records and when they used eBay to sell them, they found out it was worth more than $500! You would be amazed to know that how much an old He-man action figure is worth on eBay, or those Pokémon cards that you once used to collect but totally forgot about it. Some vintage collectors' items are worth $1000-$20000 now and if you own such rare items, thousands of dollars are just few mouse clicks away!

But all of these are just the tip of a huge iceberg. This is what people do when they want to sell second-hand items online. But eBay can offer more than that. It is a platform to build your own empire of successful c-commerce. When huge internet enthusiast Pierre had the idea of eBay (the known myth is that his wife influenced him to come up with this), his goal was to fill the gap in the market, a gap between potential buyers and seller. He wanted to build a network so that both parties can communicate to each other freely and easily without any third party in between. So he built eBay (AuctionWeb) as a level playing field where similar minded people could come and share their interests and exchange products with cash. By the time Pierre came up with eBay, he was already a successful millionaire who sold his business to Microsoft and yet to have his 30th birthday! So if you are confident and passionate enough, you can also become a successful entrepreneur, a trusted online retailer whose annual earning is a six figure digit (why not seven?). This book will guide you through a step by step process on the methods of selling, from basics to pro. You will learn secrets from already established sellers, tips, and tricks for successful selling and much more which will help you to become a super-seller in the eBay universe.

eBay: The Basics

Setting up user account

Just like any other basic sign-up, the very first thing you have to do is register at eBay. The registration is free and the whole process is very simple and straight forward. Before you start the registration, be sure you have the details of your credit card information, banks information, home address and postal code, a valid email address and your phone number. eBay is very strict on user account information so check everything after you finish filling up the forms. If any information is flagged false for some reason, eBay has the right to suspend your account and cancel all of your auctions. Be careful when you enter the credit card information because eBay uses it to check the authenticity of the identity of the users and to detect fraud.

Next thing to do is to set up user ID(with a strong password). You cannot use your email address as ID or any name that is already taken by another user. And refrain from using silly names (like D@rkLorDSam). This name will be visible to the future buyers so come up with a name that sounds professional and does not arouse any suspicion. Though eBay allows you to change you ID after 30 days but don't do it often. If you establish your name as a trusted seller, then this ID name would become a brand of its own. People will recognize the ID and will refer your ID as a trusted retailer. And when you set your password, try making it such that it can be remembered easily yet difficult to guess (in case someone tries to enter your account). There are some basic rules of setting up a secure password; it must be a mixture of lower case and upper case with numeric on it. As an example, you can use your favorite star wars character and mix it up with numbers such as Ob1WanK3n0b1. Things like these are easy to remember yet strong enough to be a secured password.

After completing the registration process, eBay will send you a confirmation email to your provided email address with a link which will activate you eBay account. Now is the time when you make your eBay account a 'Sellers Account'. A seller's account needs additional financial information such as valid credit card/debit card information and bank information. When you successfully provide this information, eBay will verify your account as 'Sellers Account' and provide you some facilities and fee options for listing your items on eBay. Currently, the first 50 listing (each month) is free with some exclusion but over 50 listings, $0.30 will apply per listing. eBay also charges final value fee per item and currently it is 10% of the total amount of the sale (Maximum fee is $750). You can also go through the other fees on selling and seller fees under the 'Help' tab on eBay website. Detailed information is given for different kinds of listings.

It might look like eBay is asking too much information from you and you might get annoyed but be assured, this is for the good of both parties, and every seller has to go through this long process so that eBay could make the transaction transparent and fraud-free. It enables everyone to be accountable for the buying-selling process. Do not worry about the information, it will be kept secured on eBay's server, and it will not be shared with the buyer or any other third party organization, not even the government. Only if there is a problem regarding a transaction (fake product or buyer didn't pay/payment bounce), then a party can apply a request for certain information (email/phone number) under the strict and valid condition, and after both parties agree, it will be available to correct the issue.

PayPal account

PayPal is the best and most secure way to do business on eBay. The major currencies are available on PayPal, and it allows both buyers and sellers to transact quickly. It is the most popular method of transaction on eBay about seven out of ten transactions is done via PayPal. In fact, it was so common among the users that on July 2002, PayPal became wholly owned subsidiary of eBay! eBay Acquired the company for $1.5 billion, and now, MasterCard is also partnered with PayPal, and there are secured card services available for users. Recently, on September 2015, they have also launched a new peer-to-peer payment service called PayPal.Me in 18 countries (including US and Canada). It will enable mobile based billing and payment services which are faster than traditional services.

There are many obvious advantages of using PayPal. eBay and PayPal are perfectly synced with each other, and you can check the status of one account on the another. While you are logged in to your eBay account, you can use the PayPal button for payment purposes and also, in the PayPal account, all the eBay transactions are clearly visible. In the near future when you are definitely going to perform regular transactions, you will be thanking yourself (and the service) that you've had opened a PayPal account and how it made your life easier. PayPal is so convenient and vastly used that often traders mark it as the only method of payment. So in the beginning, though the whole process of opening a PayPal account might seem a bit hassle but it is worth the extra time and labor.

Premium account

At the beginning of your PayPal signup process, you will be given options of types of account. It is free to open a personal account and initially this is all you need to get started. For the first few months you can do trading on eBay for free but eventually, you will definitely start trading big amounts, and you will probably have to upgrade to Premium Account. Upgrading to the Premium Account is beneficial in the long run because it will enable you to receive debit card/credit card payment for a small fee.

Note: DO NOT use the same password on PayPal as you did on eBay. Your email address might be the same but put different passwords for the two accounts. If someday, someone hacks your eBay account (it's very rare, but it happens), they will automatically get access to your PayPal account if you have the same password and the result will be catastrophic. We advise you to put different types of password this time totally unrelated to your eBay password.

Feedback

When an auction is successfully done, the buyer and the seller have the option to leave feedback for each other on eBay after the transaction is completed. Feedback is very important for the sellers because it affects the overall feedback score and the future potential buyers can see the comments left behind by the previous buyer. A good feedback point helps to build a good reputation in the online market and attracts more potential buyers. If there are other retailers selling the same product as you on eBay, but your feedback point is higher than them, buyers will definitely be interested in you. Feedback points and comments are like the example of customer service. A happy buyer/customer's good comment will benefit your business significantly. The feedback score is visible in a bracket beside the eBay user name of a seller. 'DanielSkipp (31)' –means the seller have received at least thirty-one positive feedbacks from the eBay customers. The more feedback comments you get from your customers, the more positive image you will get as a trader. The more feedback points you get, the more it gives an accurate picture of your sincerity and authenticity on eBay.

Here are the basics on how a feedback works (directly quoted from eBay Website):

Feedback scores are made up of the number of positive, negative and neutral Feedback ratings a member has received over time. In most cases, the Feedback score represents:

- +1 point for each positive rating
- No points for each neutral rating
- -1 point for each negative rating

When a seller reaches a feedback score of 10, he/she gets a yellow star. This is kind of a landmark for a new seller because unless you get a yellow star, you will not get access to special 'Buy It Now' tab at a fixed price. Later as your feedback score increases, the color of your star will change accordingly. You will gradually get a blue, turquoise, purple, red and green star and then, shooting starts after your reach more than 9999 scores!

Buyers can click on the feedback number next to your user ID anytime and get a breakdown of your transaction history. They will see all the positive, neutral and negative feedbacks that the previous buyers have left for you. You can't force a buyer to give positive feedback, and you can stop negative feedbacks by giving excellent customer service. A single line feedback comment "It didn't work!" can destroy your reputation and discourage customers to buy items from you so be careful and very supportive when you deal with a customer. The time of delivery, the quality of the product, the similarity of the product with the given image…these are the factors which lead to positive/neutral or negative feedbacks. There is, however, an option to hide your negative feedbacks but do not activate it. The 'Private' option in the feedback tab hides all the selected comments, but it creates suspicion and distrust. Customers would think there is something wrong with your trading history so they might avoid you and incline towards your competitors. After a given transaction, a feedback from a customer might take up to 90 days so don't get frustrated, if they are happy with the product; they will give you a positive feedback you just make sure you do the right thing always.

Giving feedback to the buyer

Before you give feedback to a buyer, you should consider certain things. First of all, there are arguments among the seller community that, should a seller give feedback first or the buyer? The logical reasoning is, a buyer should give feedback first because unless you are really sure that the buyer is happy with the product and gave a positive review, you shouldn't attempt to give yours. There is a possibility that you gave a positive feedback but after that, for some reason, the buyer gave a neutral one, and the mutual consent is destroyed. So try waiting a bit and give feedback to your customer after they give theirs.

From a seller's perspective, you should keep these things in mind when you give feedback to a customer:

1. Did the buyer pay quickly and used the method specified by you?
2. Did the transaction go smoothly?
3. Did they demand anything unreasonable?

Now you might wonder as a seller, what would be your feedback? You might find some cliché comments every now and then, but it does not matter. Try to be factually accurate or if you think that writing an 80 character feedback is stressful and do not have time, just write something which appears positive such as:

- The payment was fast. Excellent customer!
- He is a great buyer. Recommended!
- It was a pleasure doing business with her. Thanks!

But avoid giving feedbacks like "Nice Customer! 10/10" or "Awesome! Totally A++". These are silly and looks very unprofessional. Though there are options for removing a feedback via 'Mutual feedback withdrawal' but the process is very lengthy and frustrating. It will deduct any negative scores, but the comments will remain, so there is no point of doing it. Just regard the comments as permanent and don't rush it. Take your time and give feedback whenever you are free of work.

Dealing with negative feedback

Sooner or later, you will get a negative feedback, it's inevitable. When it happens, don't panic or get frustrated and most importantly, don't get angry and aggressive on the person who gave the negative feedback. There are several methods of tackling negative feedback. If you are a beginner and have very low feedback score, some people might advise to scrap the whole account and start from the beginning, again. Don't listen to them; one or two negative comments will not harm your business in the long run if you handle it smartly.

The best way is to focus on gaining positive feedback to counter the negative ones. Mistakes will happen at the early stage of your online career but eventually, your overall trading history is all that matters, not one or two miscommunications. The more you earn positive feedback; it will eventually outweigh the negative ones. At the early stage, one negative feedback out of ten will show 90% score, but later on, one negative out of thousand will show 100%.

Your primary target should be selling your goods and delivering it to the buyers. Somewhere on the road, you will definitely meet some buyers who are too rigid but most of the time, people ignore small issues and will not hold it against you. On the other hand, you can reply to negative feedbacks smartly, and it will be visible to others. You can click on 'reply to feedback received' at the bottom of the feedback page and add a follow-up comment. Don't be aggressive, try to be factual and appear proactive on the issue. If you explain the issue on the reply, later other customers will understand what went wrong. If the feedback is like this: "Didn't get what I expected and it took ages to deliver! Avoid this seller!!" try to be calm and reply "The item was sent from our end within 24 hours, was as described. Offered refund." Don't insult the buyer on the reply or justify yourself aggressively. Occasionally, they might come back and reply to your reply and say something bad. In that case, keep calm and reply logically. People will see who is right and who is wrong. There are options to contact the buyer via email to resolve the issue, so try it first. If you fail to resolve it, or the buyer is nor responsive, just avoid and write it down in their feedback section.

My eBay

When you become a pro, My eBay will be your best friend. Here you will see your own auctions and things you have sold till now. You will get detailed information of items you have sold (Buyers see items they want to bid on this tab). The first page is a summary of your current activity. My eBay will also show you useful selling reminders. There are other tabs such as My Message, Selling Totals, and Items I've Sold. The last tab (items I've sold) is very important when you become an active seller. This is a quick easy-to-view tab and helps you organize sending your items to the buyers. You can check if they paid for the item or even get buyers delivery address from here. In My eBay section, you will also get access to 'Dispute Console' which you can visit if you have any problems regarding any transaction. You can also access your PayPal account from My eBay page.

Getting Ready to $ell

As a newbie, you will only get to sell an item with auctions at the beginning. Once you reach 10 positive feedbacks and get a star, only then you will get to choose between sell at auction or list it as 'Buy it Now'. Before you start listing your items in order to sell them, you must learn to navigate some pages to successfully complete the listing process. Those are as follows:

Choosing the main category

The very first thing you have to do to list your item in is to select the main category. This is the top category for your items. Do not go to detailed listing categories just now, only do the basic. If you are selling some old vintage TV show DVDs, just pick the category 'DVD, Film, and TV'. You can choose the precise genre (drama,comedy) later.

Selecting the subcategory

The next thing you do is select the subcategory of your item. Suppose you are listing the collector's edition DVD of original sci-fi/horror TV show 'The Twilight Zone'. In this case, under the main category, your subcategory would be like this- DVD, Film, and TV > DVDs > TV Programs > TV Horror. How you list your item is totally up to you. Some items might have more subcategories, some few. Choose your categories wisely until you get the precise category of your product.

There is also an option in this page where you can opt to list your auction in another category. Suppose you are listing unisex clothes. You can add them under 'Men's clothing' as well as add a second category of 'Women's Clothing'. But there is a catch. If you've already used your free listings, adding a second category will double your listing fees.

If you are not sure about the subcategory of your item, try searching eBay with the relevant keyword and see if you find similar items. At the top of the auction page, you will find the breakdown information of the category information. The breakdown looks like this:

Books, Comics and Magazines > Books > Non-Fiction > History

If you are listing videos or DVDs, you can add more to your listing process which will make it easier to list them, and buyers will get more information later. If you click 'Continue' it will ask you the EAN code of your DVD, and you can just insert it in the box, and eBay will automatically fill up the description for that DVD without your input. Buyers can then see the detailed information of your movie/TV show.

Price and Item Details

On the next page, you have to choose the price for your item. You can either choose a base price for the auction or a fixed price for 'Buy it Now' option. There also a feature available on this section of eBay where you can donate a certain amount of your earnings to charity. You can choose who you donate and how much you donate from a pull-down box.

The next thing to do is to select the duration (for the auction) and a photo of your item (the First one is free). You can also choose some optional extras if you want to. There is an option to add 'visitor counter' under you listing so that people could see the popularity of your item. Interested buyers will be encouraged to bid high if they see there are many potential buyers for your item. So, think before you put it on any item. It is useful mostly for any rare collectibles.

Postage and payment methods

Though the best payment method is via PayPal but if you add more payment options, you will get a bigger audience for your item. Same applies for 'Post-to locations' option. You can select a free certificate of posting from the pull-down box under postal insurance. If you want, you can also add return policy for your item. Adding a return policy attracts customers, and it enforces your authenticity and sincerity as a seller. For special cases, you can also add payment instruction of you want to get paid within a certain time frame or only via certain method (PayPal).

Review and Submit

This is the final part of the whole process before you complete your listing. You can check every detail of your item at a glance before you submit it by clicking on 'submit listing' button at the bottom. If you accidentally clicked it and realized you have to edit it, don't worry. There are options for editing later too. You can edit your listing. If there are more than 12 hours left on your auction or no one yet bid on it. To edit your listing, follow this process:

- Go to 'My eBay'
- Select 'Selling' under 'All Selling'
- Select the item you want to edit by clicking on its auction title
- Click 'Revise your item'
- Choose the blue 'Edit' option on the right of each category
- Make your desired changes

- Click 'Save Changes' on the bottom

- Click 'Submit revisions' on the bottom

You cannot edit your listing if someone already bid on it. Instead, you can add information and the buyers will see it after you save it.

eBay Fees

There are multiple fees such as insertion fees (fee for listing an item), and final value fee (excluding taxes). A seller gets 50 free listings per month after that, insertion fees will be applicable per category. The final value fee is calculated based on the total amount of sale (original price, shipping charges and other charges). There are also optional fees such as advanced listing upgrade fees or supplemental service fees. You can explore all of their fee details here on their website:
http://pages.ebay.com/help/sell/fees.html

Think before you start selling

Before you start diving into the infinite selling opportunities on eBay, you must pause and think about what you are going to sell on eBay. You might wonder "What are the best things I can sell on eBay?" well, there is no definite answer to that question. eBay is a platform to sell anything and everything as long as it is legal. The buying trends depend on various factors: seasons, fashion, sudden popularity and so on. But the best path is to sell those items which you already know of and enjoy selling. Things you already manufacture or if you know suppliers, who can provide you with quality goods, start selling those. Researching on products and knowing the true value of a product in the market is a special ability of a seller. If you find what you want to sell and enjoy doing it, then go for it. If you play the cards right, you will definitely become the go-to guy for certain items and shine on eBay as the most trusted seller of that product. Here are some suggestions for you:

Sell Things that you're Passionate about. If you really have fun selling it then, it will not feel like working anymore. If you are passionate about fashion trends and go for clothing. Why not convert your obsession into money? Perhaps your knowledge can help you making money! If you know where to find rare comics, then become a comic seller! There are people who spend hours lurking in old book-markets and libraries. If you are like them who often finds rare comics and books, then start selling those on eBay. You will definitely get more than a fair bargain for a really rare issue comic.

Use your hobby as the driving tool. If you are a gadget enthusiast and know your stuff, then it will help you during listing. If you are familiar with the certain brand or certain models of items, then use that knowledge while you write a description of your item. The plus point is, if you have deep knowledge of something, you can spot those on garage sales, and while many people will not see the true value of it, you will see at instantly and can sell it on eBay and profit from it.

Follow the classic path of an eBay seller. First, start with your house. Clean your closet and store room and see what you can sell. You never know, some items may be worth more than you think (Those old Pokémon cards). After that look around to your friends and family's house. Eventually, you will end up in flea markets and garage sells for more items to sell. And when you become a pro, you will definitely find a wholesaler or a supplier to sell regularly on eBay.

Expand your already established business on eBay. If you already own a shop then try selling the extra good on eBay. Maybe those returned products or those overstocks. Soon you will find that selling on eBay is more profitable than selling in your tiny brick and wood shop.

Don't try to list too many different types of items. Just stick with two or three categories and start building your reputation on it. Focus on those categories which interest you more than selling 7-8 different types. Try becoming an expert on certain categories so that people recognize you on eBay as the best guy to buy that item from. Limiting categories enable you to gain knowledge on items and become a specialist on it.

Assemble a team. If you want to focus on collectibles, then assemble a small search-and-pick team who will look for rare collectibles for you. Train them by taking them with you once or twice or make a booklet of items. Eventually, they will learn what to find and where to find. If you are interested in manufactured goods or clothing, then find a supplier or wholesaler and partner with them. Your team must be built on mutual understanding. Make sure all of your team members know what you are actually looking for so that they can supply you with potential items to sell on eBay.

The smaller the better. Go for items which are small and easy to package and transport. If your items are small, it will cost less to deliver. Items like clothing and big hardware need storage space, and you have to be cautious during transportation. On top of that, there are chances of damage if the items are too big and fragile.

Business on eBay is Fun!

eBay gives you tools to research the market and various advanced tools and supplements to boost your business. eBay also helps to enhance the appearance of the product by listing it relevant information. Here are certain things you can use during your business on eBay. These will definitely help you in the long run:

Do market research. You can search eBay's completed item search to find out items on demand. It will give you insights on what to sell next or whether you should change some of your selling items according to the market demands. But don't look too much into otherwise you will be lost in information. Things like eBay Hot Items Report or specialized services like Terapeak will overwhelm you.

You don't literally have to build it from scratch. Look into research sellers like drop-off stores. They sell merchandise on eBay on behalf of their owners. Take notes on their sales and find out what the best price is and what is on demand now or which items have the highest bids. Then find those items for yourself and start auctioning.

Browse catalogs and window shop. If you are passionate about any brand then browse as many catalogs and magazines as you can. Don't be shy to do window shopping for that brand. You never know, you might find some brand never heard before at a price less than $5 and re-sell them on eBay for more than $100.

Think like the customers. Put yourself in their shoes and think if you were a buyer, what price would attract you the most? Would you buy it for $30? Is the photo good enough? Is the description of the product helpful? If any of them does not satisfy your question, then you must edit your item. You can also go through other seller's items and read their description. Do whatever they are doing but do it better!

Be patient and give yourself enough time to become an expert. Rather than spending an hour or two, spend weeks on items unless you feel confident. Become an expert on a few selected items and then focus expanding your business around those. There are people who spent almost three weeks on high-end collector's edition fountain pens and then decided to start selling. If you give yourself enough time to research then you will soon become a power seller of a few particular specialized items.

Keep an eye on completed auctions on eBay. Every couple of weeks, do a research on completed auctions. eBay keeps those data for two to three weeks max so make your own database. Compile a database of the items which attracted lots of bids and sold at high price. Try gathering more detailed information like starting bid of those items, the highest bid and whether it was sold at auction or with buy it now. After a few months, you will have a very useful database of seller's items with details and it will help you decide what to sell at what price. If you are smart enough, you will also see trends of the buyers and even see a pattern! Though it sounds far-fetched but there are people who can predict the demand shift of the market and act accordingly. If you try, you can also become one of them.

'New' and 'Like New' items get sold faster. No matter what it is, items with original boxes and wrappers attract more potential buyers. If you have price tags with it, buyers will definitely be interested in those.

Get an online appraisal service for the rare collectibles. There are services that can assess your item and give you a report of its market value. If you are going to sell a rare action figure or work of art but don't know its true value, try one of these services and send detailed photos. They will send you reports of its worth in the market, and then you can start selling it on eBay.

Get an authentication service to grade your item and certify its authenticity. For collectibles such as coins, stamps, baseball cards or rare comics, it's important to get certified for authenticity and condition. If you want to check the authenticity of a coin, go to the professional coin grading service (www.pcgs.com) or for check the condition of a rare comic, go to (www.cgccomics.com).

Go international! Do not just limit yourself within the US market. There are separate eBay sites around the world. Place an ad of your item on a foreign eBay site. Besides the English speaking eBay Canada, eBay Australia and eBay UK, you can search other versions too if you know the language, even place ads there.

Find out your competitors. If you get your items from your locality (from a wholesaler, flea market, second-hand store or garage sale), try finding others who sells products similar to you. You can easily find them by advanced searching. Go to advanced search option and select 'Items near me', check the box and choose distance (say 100 miles) and click search. Then you will see who the people selling similar items around you. Save their user ID in My eBay section and visit them regularly to check out what they are selling. Keeping an eye on your competitors is very important when you are doing business on sales.

Buy the seasonal items on sale and save it to profit later. You will find Christmas, New Year items on sale at a very low price in the beginning of January, online or in stores near you. Buy them at a bulk rate and store them in a facility till November and then sell then on eBay for profit. The Same technique can be applied to 2nd hand college textbooks and back-to-school items. Buy them in early summer and sell them in the fall. The trick is to wait till a few weeks before a holiday or the event and then start selling at a high price when demands are through the roof.

Expand your existing business on eBay. If you already have a loyal customer base at your physical shop, encourage them to visit your eBay shop. You can offer them special discounts if they buy items from you eBay store. This way you increase your feedback score and earn stars to become a great eBay seller.

Try to be friends with your local authorized dealer. If you know someone from the management of the resale shop near you, it will help you boost up your business. Let them know what you sell on eBay. Perhaps your local authorized dealer can let you sell the latest item a day before it hits the shelves and that will surely give your business an upper hand. Even putting it online hours before it hits the market would give you an obvious advantage over your competitors. Always look for such chances and opportunities.

Find merchandisers and wholesalers among your friends and family. If any of your relatives or friends is in merchandising business who can supply you goods at a cheaper price than the market, grab it now! If your uncle is with the wholesaling business, then ask him to give you discounts at a bulk price. There are people who even benefited from their in-law's business by partnering with them. You can even ask them to be your mentor and advisor if they are already in the business for a long time.

Electronic gadgets sell easily. Anything that runs on electricity and works can be sold on eBay very easily. Electronic items are one of the most popular items on eBay. If you have good sources for camera equipment, computers, audio entertainment or any other gadget, go for it! Despite the high number of sellers who mostly sells electronics, your product will definitely sell if you know your gadget properly and market it smartly.

Use your love for sports to earn money. If you love a certain sports say, soccer and you can get your hands on second-hand equipment and jerseys then you should definitely sell them on eBay. An original 2002/03 home kit of Manchester United is worth more than $200 dollars if you find the right people on eBay.

Car or Bike enthusiast? Try eBay Motors. It is solely devoted to buying and selling cars, motorbikes, parts, accessories or anything that has engines. Used parts and even repair manuals are in high demand. If you have access to any automobile junkyard and get your hands on engine or body parts then start selling them on eBay. If you know your car or your bike, you will know what to sell and what a buyer might be looking for.

Some tips and strategies

Choose the correct keywords for your item's title. The basic search of eBay looks for titles and keywords, not categories. So what you write on your title is very important. Carefully think what words the buyers might use in the search box when they are searching products that you are selling? You are allowed up to 55 characters for a title so include as many keywords as you can, don't spare a space. Important things to include are:

- Brand Name
- The product
- Size
- Color
- 'New' or 'Like New' word (if it is)
- Model

- Age (if used)

Write different sizes while selling on foreign eBay sites. There are many items (Like shoes) which size conversion is different in different countries. A US 10 shoe is UK 9 and 43 in Europe. So don't forget to write the size conversion chart in the keywords. A Nike shoe ad should look like this within 50 characters:

Original Nike Shoe / Almost New / Black / Size UK 9 / US 10 / EU 43

Don't hesitate on writing a long description. Unlike the title, description box has no limit of characters, so you write any length of description. Write long description if it is required. Do not fail to add any important information and allow the buyers to assume something. In that case, they might not bid on your item or later give negative feedback if they are not satisfied.

Write a valid reason for selling a used item. Obviously, you are not using it that's why you are selling it but a potential buyer will wonder why you are selling an item. Clearing out the reason in the description area will make the potential buyer more confident. The reasons for selling could be- 'need some space in my room' or 'just bought a new model' or 'need urgent cash'.

Write the genuine condition of your item. If you really never used an item then write 'as new'. If you still have the original box and wrapping papers then write that too on the description. If you used the item for yourself couple of times then write that information. Don't just write 'used' or 'second-hand'. Write in brief how many times you used or if there is any wear or tear on it. Try to be accurate and honest as much as you can. It does not matter if the product is scratched or slightly damaged. If your description is clear about it, a potential buyer will still be interested in buying it.

Include a story or history behind a collectible item. If you are selling something rare, write a story behind it- how you acquired it or when you got it. A good story behind a truly rare collector's edition comic book will definitely encourage a buyer and reinforce its authenticity.

Mention the color in the description in detail. Don't just write 'Blue' even if there is a photo of your item. Things appear different in photos under different lights. Blue is a vague term, write what kind of blue it is- Cyan Blue, Ocean Blue, Navy Blue or Sky Blue. Later people might accuse you of delivering wrong colored product if you do not mention the color correctly.

Be creative and write a sales pitch! Just like the old days when door-to-door salesmen used to say wonderful things about the product they are selling; you can also do write fantastic stuff about your item. Write how excellent the quality is, how you never saw such condition of a product or how you enjoyed every moment of using it! Though sometimes it sounds over the top, people still likes interesting sales pitch.

Don't dare to list an item without a photo. Photos are extremely important when it comes to selling something on eBay. Use a good, high-quality camera to get a nice snap of your item. Nowadays even smartphones have a 13-megapixel camera with it and are very good for object photography if you get the lights right.

Invest on commercial mannequins if you are selling clothes. People prefer seeing a photo of a mannequin wearing the dress rather than drooping it on a gray hanger. Sometimes they prefer real people wearing it, in that case, ask one of your good looking friends to pose for you wearing that dress. Don't take a selfie wearing the dress, it does not properly show the dimensions. It's better to take a photo of your friend wearing the dress under daylight or bright white light.

Use 7 or 10 days listing instead of 1 or 3 days listing. One day listings are suspicious because people tend to think that there is something wrong with the product, and that's why the seller is in a hurry. And also, one day is not enough for buyers to search for your item. Do not use 3 days listing unless you are desperate for cash, moving to another location or have some kind of deadline looming. Seven days is the most popular auction time because it will finish at the same time and date as it started and it will be visible throughout the week. Even if someone only logs in once a week, he/she will still see it. Use 10 days listing if you are selling something big like car or motorbike. 10 days are helpful for a big item because it spans two weekends, and the potential buyer might visit you and have a look at the product before buying it. If they see the item on Sunday, they can visit you on the next Sunday and confirm the purchase.

Don't focus too much on scheduling. Usually, people log into eBay on Sundays, but you should spread out your tasks and activities throughout the week to build on volume of items. Spreading out also helps to package your items otherwise every Monday, you will lose time solely on packaging and delivering your products.

Always check the system status announcement board for any schedule maintenance or update. Get an early heads-up and schedule your work beforehand if there is any system offline imminent. Always watch out for any service problems or scheduled interruptions.

Save time with Turbo Lister. Turbo lister is eBay's own free, fast and easy listing tool which allows you to build professional-looking listing very quickly and efficiently and you can edit them in bulk. This feature enables you to duplicate listings to save time and also create templates for similar kinds of products. The standard information remains the same in a common template, so you don't have to write every time you list a bulk product (like clothes). This is useful if you have vast ranges of products or similar type of items. Usually, if you are selling more than a thousand items only, then it can be useful. Turbo Lister allows you to list and upload up to 3000 products in one click. You can also schedule your listing via Turbo Lister. Don't forget to keep a backup of your turbo lister. Make sure you regularly update your backup. The backup is generally saved in 'My Documents' on your computer.

A Few Insights and secrets from established sellers

1. Buyers demand easy payment options. The most popular options are- PayPal, Credit Card, Electronic Check and Money Order.

2. More than 70% of eBay users use PayPal.

3. People will trust you more if they know you have your own Merchant Account.

4. Use reply templates designed for responding typical queries from the buyers, it saves a lot of time.

5. Don't just send the reply template, try using the person's name on the top so that it looks like you read their mail and responded accordingly.

6. Never delete an email. Never. Throwing away and deleting an email completely can back and haunt you. Keep it for future references.

7. Honesty is the best policy. Be clear about your product on the description and contact with the customer if you face a problem during delivery. It will help you to avoid any negative feedback.

8. Don't hold personal checks as policy.

    Most eBayers are honest and bouncing checks are the result of carelessness. Let them know and wait for them to correct it.

9. Start with a low bidding price if you know that an item is going to sell for sure. This will get you a healthy bidding and attract more crowds.

10. Use packaging and delivery services like UPS to save time and money.

11. Picture says it all. Take a good photo of your item with all of its aspects, even faults and cracks to make it more credible.

12. Send thank you notes and receipt email to your customers every time they make payments. Give them you email ID if they need to contact in the future and ask them to give a good feedback in your email. Nine out of ten times, this gesture will help you to get nice positive fccdbacks.

13. When you list an item, make sure your description is as complete as possible. Leave no stone unturned or it might attract wrong bidders. Do not neglect to put a crucial information of the item.

14. Do not overcharge for shipping. Buyers are very sensitive about this and any kind of misunderstanding might lead to negative feedback.

15. Be cautious when you decide to leave negative feedback on a buyer's ID who deserves it. Try to find solutions before you jump into putting negative feedbacks or else, they might take revenge on you.

16. Treat your customers like royalty and they will reward you with loyalty.

17. Use the delivery confirmation service. Some buyers might demand refund though you did your part. With some extra fees, you can track the product and send this information to the receiver to keep transparency of the process.

18. Double check your title for any spelling errors. eBay mainly focuses on the title and buyers search it with keywords so be careful about it. Use spell checker add-ins like Grammarly if needed.

19. Customers are always right; don't tell them otherwise.

20. Always underpromise and over deliver.

21. Follow up on a customer after a week to check if they are satisfied.

22. Include shipping costs in the descriptions.

23. Don't forget to insure your package and pack it well and tight.

24. Keep your auctions going till the last second; don't end it early unless someone offered you an insane amount.

25. Always be clear and avoid any kind of misunderstanding with the customer.

26. Items highlighted in bold fonts are 50% more likely to sell fast. Try it now.

27. Talk to the high bidders on the phone if possible. Email travel at light speed but talking is more effective.

28. Save your my eBay page monthly to track your sales totals. File this for income tax records

29. All Prices are in USD so be careful when you deal with foreign orders.

30. Use asterisks on your special collectible items. Feature them like this-
    **** ANCIENT COINS ****

31. Find your niche. You can't just sell anything and everything. Try focusing only those item which you are good at selling

32. Murphy's Law is always lurking! Don't forget to keep a backup of everything.

33. Use good sales policies to avoid any kind of trouble. Put terms and condition on every listing you make including shipping conditions, payment methods, packaging insurance, etc.

The secrets of branding and marketing

Every successful businessman spends enough time behind branding their products and marketing their goods to attract and retain customers. Unless you are the only seller of your type of product, you will be competing with other sellers on eBay, maybe hundreds even thousands like you. The only way to stand out it via branding your products differently and uniquely. You will have to make your items noticeable among thousands of similar items. How do you do it? You do it with clever marketing. Make sure that you market your product to your desired customer demographic. If its electronic gadgets, the photo must attract a tech-savvy individual. If it's a clothing line, you must be able to attract trendy and fashionable people.

Most of the hard works on eBay are already done for you. But you can do more on Branding if you use some additional features. If you really want to put your products up high, the best way to do it is to use eBay store. It allows you to display all of your products together under one branded area of your company's

name. Buyers can click on your brand area and see what products you have on eBay at a glance. You should make enough time to design a dynamic, stylish and attractive eBay store for your brand. It's all about making a name,

making a brand of your own in the eBay universe.

If you subscribe to an eBay store, it will be available in My eBay, and you can access it design the functionality of your store. You can click on 'Store Deign' tab and use HTML (web

designing language) to design an attractive eBay store. You can also choose your own theme and layout for the store. You can choose up to 300 store categories to display your products under different categories.

The best way to do marketing is via email marketing. eBay allows you to mail your customers for free so you should take benefit of it. You can send up to 100 emails at once to your customers. Go to 'Marketing tools' and select 'email marketing' under 'store marketing'. Here you have the opportunity to create and send 100 emails each month. Create an eye-catching email of latest offers and discounts and send to 100 potential customers or loyal customers. You can also send welcome emails to new potential buyers. Use HTML or email layouts to make it more interesting and flashy.

Staying safe from scams

As a whole, eBay is a safe platform to do business uninterrupted. But inevitably, there will be people who will try to misuse the platform and con people. Here are some of the common scams that you should avoid:

Fake Emails

You might get fake emails with strange requests claiming that it is from eBay but before opening, you must check eBay's latest safety information and updates.

Phishing

The scammer will try to convince you that the email notification is real by using eBay logos. They might ask for sensitive bank information or credit card information. These phishing spams typically threaten to close down your account or give some kind of warnings. They even use eBay's original terms and conditions link. You must be able to detect these to stay safe.

Alternate methods of payments

Never agree on any other payment methods other than eBay approved methods. Never use instant money transfer services like western Union or MoneyGram. These payment methods are highly risky and unsafe.

Any Dealing Off eBay

eBay can only protect your money and products if the transactions are made on eBay. Otherwise, any deals outside eBay will be totally up to the seller's consent. If the buyer emails the seller and the deal/transaction is done outside eBay, no party can hold eBay accountable if something goes wrong; though the listings might have been done on eBay.

Conclusion

There is no ultimate truth or divine revelation on how to become a successful eBay seller. Only those who are passionate and have the real business mindset can shine on eBay. You should be realistic and very practical about your business ideas. You have to ensure that you will get the best price and the supply of your products will be secured all the time. Every now and then, you have to switch your interest according to the market demand to stay competitive. Don't stop researching and keep enough profit margins to feed your business and expand it if needed. Try to compete with other sellers through your customer service, price and branding skills. Always follow eBay's rules and regulations and do not attempt to violate any of those. Try to learn from other sellers. Watch what they are doing and do it better than them. Learn from successful sellers and collect tips from them. Try to explore new features and possibilities on eBay every now and then. No one will guarantee you a 100% success rate, only YOU can make it happen with confidence and efforts. Never stop striving for more; Never stop selling more.

BEFORE YOU GO

If you liked this book, you may like these other books from Mark Thomas

Check out more books by Mark Thomas

Chapter One – The Money Mindset

Before you even begin to think about making over ten thousand dollars in a month in just ninety days, you have to know what the proper mindset is in order to achieve that goal. You see, your mindset is extremely important to what you want to achieve. If you tell yourself you can't do something, then you won't be able to achieve it! So let's explore how you can have the proper money mindset in order to get rich!

First, let's take a look at an example of someone who has a money mindset and someone who doesn't. We'll take a look at two handymen. Handyman one, let's call him George, walks into a home and he is approached by the homeowner. The homeowner tells him or her they want crown molding put in their upstairs bathroom. George affably agrees it will make the appearance of their home nicer, but that's it.

Now, the second handyman's name is Josh. Josh walks into the home and he approaches the homeowner who tells him about wanting the crown molding. Josh also agrees it will look nicer, but he also goes on to explain how the crown molding will improve the value of the home over the long run.

Do you see the difference? George just wanted to make the home look better for aesthetic purpose only, but Josh saw the *value* in putting the crown molding in from an investment standpoint.

Being able to see the value in something is the money mindset. There are numerous other aspects to the money mindset, so let's take a look at them.

#1 Mindful of the Long-Term

There are many people out there who are looking to make money fast, but they rarely ever make a lot of it because of greed. Their first mindset is to think about what's in it for them. Rather, they should be thinking about how they can add as much value to someone else first. For example, it's like building credits with someone or an organization over the long-term. You might never need to use those credits, but if you do, help is returned in abundance. Don't allow your short-term greed destroy your long-term wealth.

#2 You Deserve Only What You've Earned

There is no room for an attitude of entitlement for someone when they have a money mindset. Don't expect to get to the corner office without paying your dues. At sixty-three years old, the man who put up the crown moldings is a great example of someone who doesn't expect something. He comes in with a good attitude to his job, does it well, cleans up, and leaves.

#3 You Believe You Deserve to be Wealthy

Money is out there for anyone to get their hands on. Once you believe you deserve to have that money, you'll subconsciously change your actions to make it happen. Stop feeling guilty about earning six figures in a year. There are people out there who earn seven and drive their companies into the ground to do it! Your mindset should not be 'why me' but 'why *not* me'? With the belief that you deserve to be wealthy too, your income will soar!

#4 You Ask Yourself What the Value of The Product or Service is Before You Spend a Dollar

People who have the money mindset are very value aware. Since they realize how hard it is to make money, they are much more careful about spending their money than the average person. They have to ask whether one dollar spent might return that dollar in the future. They are on the lookout for great deals and tend not to feel buyer's remorse because they purchase things that have a greater value than what they paid.

#5 You're Always Looking for Synergies and Leverage

When you go out to play tennis with people at a club or you're hanging out with some new friends, get excited! There could be synergies involved with those people. Not only are you having a good time with those people, but you are parlaying your relationship right into an excellent business opportunity. A website is an excellent example of leveraging assets to earn more. Besides earning advertising money, you can earn money by selling products and services. Your website can also serve as an online resume PR hub if you want to do more public works. If you haven't started a website, you really ought to!

#6 You Realize a Dollar Spent Today Could Grow To Much More In The Future

People who have the money mindset are naturally frugal. They despise letting go of too much money because they've already figured out what they spent today might have turned into if they had saved and invested at a ten percent rate of return over the following five to thirty years. Compound growth anchors money mindset people into spending less than they have earned. With an aggressive savings rate, you'll be surprised with just how much you could accumulate in a 401k in ten years.

#7 You're All About Tax Optimization

It's imperative to think about how much you have to earn before purchasing a particular item due to taxes. A car that costs $21,000 requires you to actually earn $30,000 in gross income. In terms of making money, someone who has a money mindset will look to reduce their taxes by figuring out the most tax friendly way they can make money passively, such as dividends. They also look to synergize their expenses if they are a freelancer or small business. There's no reason to do a company offsite in North Dakota if you can do one in Kauai. Figuring out how to pay little or no taxes becomes a hobby for someone with a money mindset.

#8 You Believe Excuses are No Excuse

You're either going to make it happen or you're going to fail. Failure is just fine; just don't make excuses and not do something about it. Figure out the reasons why you failed and then try again until you succeed. You need to believe you deserve only what you've earned, you take ownership for your failures and you most past them. Excuses are for those who blame the world for their shortcomings rather than themselves. The more excuses you use, the less you believe you are able to make things happen on your own.

#9 You Never Fail Due to a Lack of Effort

You can fail because your competition is incredibly talented, there was bad timing, or a natural disaster happened, but you will never fail due to a lack of doing your best. There are many people out there who say they are going to make a living writing or freelance programming, but most of them won't even send a draft of what they're writing to someone else for feedback. They don't want to put in the time to make the money.

#10 You Execute Solutions

Recognizing a problem or coming up with an idea is one thing. Coming up with the solution is more important. There are so many people out there who like to point out injustices or complain about something, but none of them doing anything about the situation. Someone with the money mindset will find a way to get it done and make it better.

If you read through this chapter, and you believe you don't have the money mindset, don't despair! Anyone can develop the money mindset. The first step is to know you're worth it and believing that you deserve to be wealthy. If you put in the effort, there is no reason you can't be enjoying that passive income flow, too.

Now that you know what the money mindset is and you know where you have to change in order to become wealthy with passive income let's look at the amazing ways you can make ten thousand dollars in a month in just ninety days!

Chapter Two – Making Money as a Coach

Are you currently struggling to make money with your coaching business but you have an expectation to make ten thousand dollars a month? Stop struggling! It's absolutely possible to make six figures a year coaching business, and it can happen pretty fast if you follow the necessary steps you need in order to fill your e-mail list and focus on getting more calls.

These are the top tips for making ten thousand dollars a month or more in as little as ninety days. That doesn't mean it's going to happen overnight easily. Building a business takes some focus and some effort. The goal is to build relationships and help the ideal client solve specific problems they're facing, and you're the coach and mentor that can help them with the problem.

The first step is developing that money mindset. Having the right mindset is extremely important when it comes to almost anything in your life. Making a consistent ten thousand dollars a month is not an exception.

You can create a vision board in order to visualize your goal. Just cut out some pictures and words from a favorite magazine and add them to a pinboard. You can also create an online one with Pinterest that's private and filled with inspiring images and quotes!

Once you've developed the mindset, you need to test those coaching packages.

Test the Packages

Market research is the core principle of making a thriving coaching package and coaching business. Don't make a package you believe will sell. Create a package based off what your ideal client actually desires.

In the first module of testing your packages, you need to ask detailed questions of your target market to be sure you are going to make packages that will actually sell. Don't skip this step! Make your market research your priority.

If you already have packages that are not selling, then find out why. Ask the ideal client what they would like to see added to the package or if there is anything else you can help them with. Change your copywriting in order to put an emphasis on the benefits and allow the readers know exactly what they can expect to occur if they work with you.

Price the Packages

In order to bring your income goals to life, you need to price your services and packages accordingly. Many coaches undercharge for their services. But if you want to be someone who goes to exotic locations and has financial freedom, then you need to create a premium coaching package!

Perhaps the thought of charging more for your package frightens you. If this is the case, keep working on your money mindset and remind yourself that your services are worth it for your clients.

Making a good income from what you do for a living will help you not only have a happy, healthy life, but it will help you be of a greater service to your clients. You'll have more income you can invest in your education as a coach, which will help you keep enhancing your skills.

Here are the following action steps you should follow in this section:

1. Figure out how many of your current coaching packages you have to sell in order for you to make the ten thousand dollars a month.

2. Ask yourself if you are undercharging. If you are, increase your rates and make new packages.

3. Work on your money mindset and beliefs if you are bumping against statements like *I can't charge that much*. It's not your packages that are the problem, it's you.

Lead Generation

Ads are an excellent way to generate leads. In fact, they're so important when it comes to growing a coaching business that they are one of the essential keys to financial freedom! Try some Facebook or Google ads for your coaching business and you'll see it increase.

There are other ways you can generate leads, too, such as going through a guest post, doing a webinar, joint ventures, and teleclasses.

Whatever you choose to begin with, keeping going with it! Make sure to keep your efforts going so that your list grows with those are interested in getting to know you and the services you provide.

Here are the actions steps that will lead you to success!

1. Create some sort of lead generating strategy. How many leads to you require coming in so that you can hit ten thousand dollars a month? How many discovery or strategy sessions do you need to have to sign the number of clients you need in order to result in ten thousand dollars a month?

2. Invest time and learning in how to run Facebook ads or pay an expert to set them up for you.

3. Read and post on how to do a webinar.

4. Begin using Facebook ads or Google ads to promote your first webinar or opt-in gift.

Consistent Marketing

A successful coach will not flip-flop when it comes to their business. They will be consistent in marketing and expanding their reach. Ask yourself how consistent you are with marketing when it comes to your business. Are you in touch with your e-mail subscribers on a regular basis? What can your readers expect from a blog or newsletter? How do your readers feel about your brand and what are they learning from you?

Consistent marketing and lead generation helps you obtain more clients and hit your ten thousand dollar a month income. It's not rocket science. It's a formula that successful coaches and marketers have been following for some time.

Here are your action steps for continuous marketing.

1. Consider hiring a virtual assistant or hiring and intern for a few hours a week so you can focus on client generation activities.

2. Focus on some money making activities, such as getting leads, booking discovery calls, marketing, and much more. E-mail your list of contacts three times a week with one newsletter and two solo e-mails. Solo e-mails are the ones you send out that have a single call to action. It usually has something to do with income generation.

Check out more books by Mark Thomas

Thank you again for downloading this book!

If you enjoyed this book, then I'd like to ask you for a favor, would you be kind enough to leave a review for this book on Amazon? It'd be greatly appreciated!

Thank you and good luck! ☺

-Mark Thomas

www.ingramcontent.com/pod-product-compliance
Lightning Source LLC
Chambersburg PA
CBHW060408190526
45169CB00002B/813